A FOREST OF TREES
DOES NOT GROW THERE IN ROWS

To Will,
with best wishes!
Follow the turtle!
Nina Wolpe

NINA WOLPE
illustrations by **ANNETTE CABLE**

SC & FC PUBLICATIONS • INTERLOCHEN, MICHIGAN

To the memory of Grandpa Chapman, who planted peanuts for the joy of a grandchild's discovery.
To my son Mike, who plants the joy of music in our hearts.
To family Dogbeings Victor, Sunshine, Bunky, Nosey, Bisi, Ginnie, Bailey, Dakota Jackson, Sushi, and Thunder,
who over the last sixty years scattered the seeds of love.

© 2014 Nina Wolpe

Published by SC & FC Publications, Interlochen, Michigan
scfcpub@gmail.com

Publisher's Cataloging-in-Publication Data
Wolpe, Nina.
A forest of trees does not grow there in rows / by Nina Wolpe ;
illustrated by Annette Cable. – Interlochen, MI : SC & FC Publications, 2014.

p. ; cm.

Summary: The book teaches children how a forest of trees grows in nature.

ISBN13: 978-0-9860794-0-5

1. Forests and forestry--Juvenile literature. 2. Trees--Juvenile literature. I. Title. II. Cable, Annette, ill.

SD376.W65 2014
634.9—dc23   2014910703

Project coordination by Jenkins Group, Inc.   •   www.BookPublishing.com

cover and interior design by Yvonne Fetig Roehler

Printed in the United States by Worzalla Publishing, First Printing, July 2014
18 17 16 15 14 • 5 4 3 2 1

A forest of trees

does not grow there in rows.

Come on!

Let's go see how it grows and grows.

All higglety pigglety,
here and now there,
like the beard on Dad's face,
like, "Yikes! Let's brush your hair."

Like the ocean seaweed
with no rhyme but with reason,
So lush, thick or thin,
and through any old season.

How does this all happen—

This forest of trees

all messy, all lovely—
What a good mystery!

A book will sure help us.
It says on page twenty
that scientists know
about forests. Know plenty.

They know how a forest
grows wild and scattered.
They know how a seed falls
and why that seed matters.

A bird will fly high.
Drop pine seeds from its beak.
Or a wind will blow tree seeds
around for a week.

A squirrel gets hungry.
She gathers acorns.
She eats some. She stores some.
Drops some in the thorns.

A few more tree seeds
get stuck on Thunder's tail.
They fall in the weeds
as he sniffs down a trail.

These seeds land behind him,
or maybe beside-y.
There's no law or order.
No rows. Nothing tidy.

These seeds shoot out roots
as they drink from rain showers.
Their trunks pop right out.
Their branches form bowers.

Some trees get so tall.

They grow wide and make shade.

The small trees beneath

get no sun, so they fade.

They wither and plop
on the ground in a pile.
A rabbit, her five kits
hide in it a while.

One fine tree but old tree
has seen its last year.
It falls with a "Crash!"
Scatters seeds there and here.

In eighty-nine years
that old tree saw no row.
Not one person came out
to the forest to hoe.

No person dug holes
forty inches apart.
No person brought seedlings
to plant from a cart.

In nature a forest
is messy and wild.
No trees grow in rows
like our carrots. Right, Child?

Laid out like a garden
with rows neat and clean?
Filled with beets and blueberries,
brown 'taters and beans?

But WAIT! What is THIS?
ROWS AND ROWS OF TALL TREES?

Two long strides apart,
planted neat as you please?

How'd it happen? Who did it?
Why? What for? And When?
This just is NOT NATURE—
a woods made by MEN???

To the library, quickly!
Let's look in more books.
It might be by magic,
the way these trees look.

We found it—the truth—
on page one hundred three.
The men in our land
needed work, so you see ...

They all came together.

They were paid to go plant

all those beautiful trees.

They sang work songs and chants.

It made the work easy.

It made the days go.

They spent months planting trees

in their row after row.

The men, strong and young,
all went home in the end.
They had earned enough money.
They'd made many a friend.

They found jobs and built homes.
They had children and wives.
They bought food and bought clothes.
Most lived comfortable lives.

They left behind rows
of these trees strong and tall.
Eighty years growing here
winter, spring, summer, fall.

Imagine the eagles,
the turkeys and bees,
woodpeckers and Deer Ones
all glad for these trees.

Strong sisters
and brothers,

bold nephews
and nieces

build tree houses,
swings,

and climb ropes in
nice breezes.

With their books, lights,
and friends,

up the tree trunks
they creep.

Have a drink, have a snack,
have a very good sleep.

A few rows are gone now.
New houses have come
to be nestled between them.
But still, there are some.

These trees make a forest

that grows in straight rows.

It isn't by nature.

Men planted it so.

THE END

ABOUT THE AUTHOR

NINA WOLPE taught for twenty years in the American Department of Defense base schools in Germany and Japan. Over another seventeen years, she taught adult education classes in Montgomery County, Maryland, and taught in Massachusetts, Illinois, and Virginia elementary schools. For two years, she lived and taught in multinational classrooms in Nigeria. She was the author of a by-lined newspaper column in the 1980s for papers in Michigan. She was married to U.S. Congressman Howard E. Wolpe and has one fabulous son, Michael Stevenson Wolpe. *A Forest of Trees Does Not Grow There in Rows* is her first picture book for children. Ms. Wolpe lives on a meadow surrounded by woods and forest in Interlochen, Michigan. She has two Turkish Van cats, Bridget Bunny Mary Sometimes Rosemary and Whitney Winnie Annie.

ABOUT THE ILLUSTRATOR

ANNETTE CABLE is a freelance illustrator and children's art teacher in Louisville, Kentucky. She lives with her husband Mark, also an artist, her daughter Izzy, a dog, four cats, and a guinea pig. You can see more of her art at *annettecable.com*.